Publications of the

MINNESOTA HISTORICAL SOCIETY

RUSSELL W. FRIDLEY, *Editor in Chief*

JUNE DRENNING HOLMQUIST, *Assistant Director for Research and Publications*

MINNESOTA HISTORIC SITES PAMPHLET SERIES, NO. 7

A LIVING PAST

15 Historic Places in Minnesota

Drawings by Ron Hunt   *Text by Nancy Eubank*

REVISED EDITION

MINNESOTA HISTORICAL SOCIETY · ST. PAUL · 1978

Library of Congress Cataloging in Publication Data

Hunt, Ron, 1934–
    A living past: 15 historic places in Minnesota.

    (Minnesota historic sites pamphlet series, no. 7)
(Publications of the Minnesota Historical Society)
    1. Minnesota — Historic houses, etc. 2. Historic sites — Minnesota. I. Eubank, Nancy. II. Minnesota Historical Society. III. Title. IV. Series. V. Series: Minnesota Historical Society. Publications.
F607.H86   917.76'03'05s   [917.76'03]   73-6721
ISBN 0-87351-077-1

CONTENTS

INTRODUCTION

The fifteen historic places in this booklet are administered by the
Minnesota Historical Society as part of the state's living past. All are
open to the public. All were carefully preserved or restored to give today's
nuclear man a glimpse of his past — a sense of where he has come from.
Each site has been associated with people, Indian as well as white, and
events that have in diverse ways written important chapters in the state's
history.

The black and white drawings in this booklet are the work of artist
Ron Hunt, a native of Dodge County who lives and works in the pictur-
esque village of Mantorville in southeastern Minnesota. They were
commissioned especially for this booklet, and the originals are owned by
the Minnesota Historical Society.

The descriptive text accompanying the drawings was written by Nancy
Eubank, who serves on the society's staff as supervisor of interpretation
for its historic sites.

Minnesota Historical Society

St. Paul, Minnesota

RUSSELL W. FRIDLEY
Director

MINNESOTA STATE CAPITOL

MINNESOTA STATE CAPITOL

"This chaste and noble building, the chief ornament of its kind in the state," as one historian called it, has been a St. Paul landmark since its completion in 1904. It was designed in the Italian Renaissance style by Cass Gilbert, a young St. Paul architect who later moved to New York and designed such well-known structures as the United States Supreme Court Building in Washington, D.C., and the Woolworth skyscraper in New York City.

Dominated by what is believed to be the largest self-supporting marble dome in the world, the capitol is 223 feet high, 433 feet in length, and 228 feet wide. Foundations, steps, and terraces are of St. Cloud granite; superstructure and dome are gray-white Georgia marble. Above the south façade are six emblematic statues and a quadriga of four horses and three human figures entitled "The Progress of the State." All these figures were the work of Daniel Chester French and Edward Potter, eminent American sculptors at the turn of the century.

Focal point of the impressive interior is the rotunda. In the floor at its base is a bronze, eight-point star symbolizing the North Star State; each two points of the star form the letter "M." Hanging from the dome is a crystal chandelier lighted by nearly a hundred bulbs. Interior walls are of polished Minnesota limestone, and many other kinds of Minnesota stone as well as twenty different types of imported marble are used in the pillars and balustrades, fireplaces, and decorative floor patterns. The woodwork is mahogany and Minnesota white oak.

Gilbert supervised both the construction and the interior decoration of the capitol, and he insisted that works of painting and sculpture be obtained from the best artists working in America at that time. All the works of art relate symbolically or historically to the state, including the well-known paintings of Minnesota's Civil War regiments which hang in the governor's reception room. Portraits of Minnesota's governors are hung in the first-floor corridors.

The Minnesota Historical Society, which is responsible for the preservation of the art and historical aspects of the building, provides guided tours of the capitol. They offer information about the state's history and government as well as about the art and architecture of this beautiful building — one of the outstanding state capitols in the nation.

Located at Cedar Street and Aurora Avenue in St. Paul; accessible from Interstate highway no. 94, Marion Street exit. Open year round.

HISTORIC FORT SNELLING

During the War of 1812, the United States found itself fighting not only the British but also numerous Indians living in the western territories and influenced by British fur traders. After the war, the U.S. government took steps to secure its western frontier and to bring the profitable fur trade under control of American traders by establishing a line of forts along the Mississippi River and some of its tributaries. Fort Snelling, established in 1819, was the northwesternmost of these posts.

For nearly thirty years the army and the government's Indian agent at Fort Snelling regulated the fur traders, confiscated liquor brought in by the traders, tried to keep white settlers off Indian lands, and attempted to make peace among warring Indian groups. To carry out these formidable tasks, various infantry, artillery, and dragoon units of the United States Army were stationed at the fort — a garrison of up to 350 men plus the women and children who accompanied them. The soldiers also functioned as stonecutters, masons, and carpenters until the fort was completed in 1824, and as farmers, woodcutters, and sawmill operators. There was little time for drill, and fortunately there was no need for fighting, since no foreign power actively challenged American authority and the Indian people of the area remained friendly.

Today, Historic Fort Snelling stands restored and rebuilt, an outpost of the past guarding the confluence of the Minnesota and Mississippi rivers from its commanding location on the bluff above. Within its formidable stone walls stand the first school and Protestant church, the first hospital, and the first permanent stone dwelling built in Minnesota. During the summer months, guides dressed in uniforms and costumes of the 1820s demonstrate many of the tasks of frontier garrison life — cooking, baking, blacksmithing, carpentry, drill, and standing guard. The restored sutler's store is open for business, and a fife and drum corps plays authentic military music. Exhibits in the long barracks explain the fort's role on the frontier and the life of the regular army soldier in the nineteenth century. Special tours, lectures, demonstrations, and publications add to the visitor's understanding of this imposing fortification that laid the foundations for white settlement in Minnesota.

Located in Fort Snelling State Park south of the Twin Cities; accessible from state highways nos. 5 and 55. Open daily during the summer.

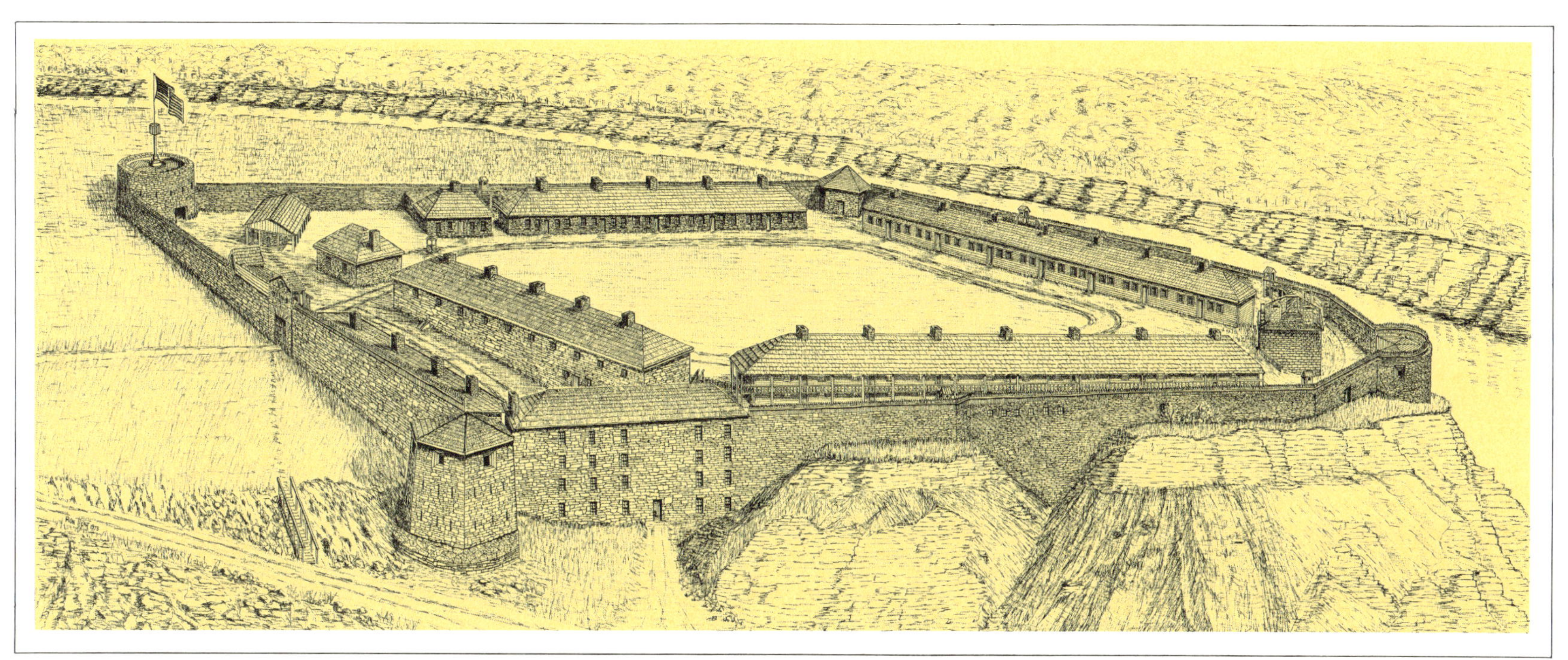

HISTORIC FORT SNELLING

ALEXANDER RAMSEY HOUSE

Alexander Ramsey was one of Minnesota's leading citizens when he built his "Mansion House" in 1872. He had arrived in the newly organized territory twenty-three years before, appointed governor by President Zachary Taylor as a reward for his help in carrying Pennsylvania for the Whigs in the 1848 election. The hearty, practical Ramsey, appreciating the opportunities of a frontier territory, promptly plunged into real estate investment and civic activities that were to make him both rich and respected in his new home. In 1855 he was mayor of St. Paul; by 1857 he estimated his wealth as "perhaps a million." He became second governor of the state in 1860, and he served for twelve years as a United States senator. Later he was to be appointed secretary of war in the cabinet of President Rutherford B. Hayes.

The big limestone house which the Ramseys built in the then elegant Irvine Park district of St. Paul reflected their wealth and position, but it also mirrored "bluff Alex's" character as a "man who wasted no time on fanciful projects." It is a comfortable home of fifteen rooms, furnished in the solid and ornamented style popular with Victorians who had come successfully through the hardships of frontier settlement and civil war. Although it seems elaborately decorated to most modern eyes, the Ramsey House is actually restrained when compared with other Victorian interiors. The Ramseys retained some of the furnishings in Sheraton and Hepplewhite styles which they had brought with them from Pennsylvania years before.

Members of the Ramsey family lived in the house until 1964, changing it little over nearly a century. Most of the original furnishings which Mrs. Ramsey selected in New York for her new home are still in the house. The ornate wooden carriage house was rebuilt at its former site in 1970 using the original plans. It serves as a visitors' center and gift shop.

Located at 265 South Exchange Street, St. Paul. Open year round.

ALEXANDER RAMSEY HOUSE

BURBANK-LIVINGSTON-GRIGGS HOUSE

As America changed in the nineteenth century from a frontier to an industrial society, businessmen successful beyond their wildest dreams in an era before income taxes built stately homes on fashionable streets all over the nation. Summit Avenue in St. Paul became the Upper Midwest's symbol of this new elegance.

The Burbank-Livingston-Griggs House, completed in 1863, was one of the earliest Summit Avenue mansions. James C. Burbank, whose family lived in the house until 1884, built a financial empire based on stagecoach and steam packet lines which enjoyed a virtual monopoly in early Minnesota. Subsequent owners of the house included retail merchant George R. Finch, Northern Pacific Railroad vice-president Thomas F. Oakes, and broker and railroad builder Crawford Livingston.

The house is an American Victorian version of an Italian villa — a style sometimes called "American Bracketed" because of the lavish ornamentation of the roof brackets at the cornices. The interior was originally finished with the heavily carved woodwork popular with Victorians, which can still be seen in the entrance and upper halls. All other interior rooms underwent extensive remodeling in the 1930s, when Mrs. Theodore Wright Griggs, daughter of the Crawford Livingstons, installed complete rooms imported from Europe within the shell of the Summit Avenue house. Most of these rooms are seventeenth- and eighteenth-century Italian or French decor complete with appropriate furnishings and art objects. The glass-walled entertainment room in the basement is an exception. It is a superior example of 1930s modern taste, with piped-in sound system and indirect lighting, both advanced ideas for the time.

Mrs. Griggs's daughter, Mrs. Jackson Burke, gave the house to the Minnesota Historical Society in 1968. In addition to regular tours during visiting hours, the house is frequently used for classes in interior design, community events, social activities, and special exhibits.

Located at 432 Summit Avenue, St. Paul. Open year round.

BURBANK-LIVINGSTON-GRIGGS HOUSE

MINNEHAHA DEPOT

This ornate little Victorian station, with its gingerbread trim and bright maroon and harvest gold colors, was affectionately known as "The Princess" to Milwaukee Road men. Located at one of the three stops on the first railroad line built out of Minneapolis, it was erected in the 1870s at a time when this line connected Minneapolis with Chicago and the East.

After a direct route between Minneapolis and St. Paul was constructed in 1880, commuters to downtown Minneapolis and visitors to Minnehaha Falls and Longfellow Zoological Gardens kept Minnehaha station busy for nearly eighty years. Hundreds came daily to board trains for the sixteen-mile, five-cent ride downtown (three trains made eight round trips daily in 1910). During war years — beginning with the Spanish-American War and including World War II — soldiers worked alongside railroad men to handle trainloads of military supplies shipped in and out of Fort Snelling three miles to the southeast.

The Milwaukee Road closed Minnehaha station in 1963 and presented the depot to the Minnesota Historical Society the following year. It has since been completely restored to its 1890s appearance by the society and the Minnesota Transportation Museum organization. On Sunday afternoons during the summer, guides are on hand to greet visitors at this charming site where Victorian ladies and gentlemen and their excited children once set out for a picnic in the park or a visit to the zoo.

Located at Minnehaha Avenue and East Forty-ninth Street across from Minnehaha Park in Minneapolis. Open Sunday afternoons from Memorial Day through Labor Day.

MINNEHAHA DEPOT

W. W. MAYO HOUSE

The founder of one of Minnesota's most famous families, William W. Mayo, built this small house in Le Sueur in 1859. There he practiced medicine for nearly five years before moving to Rochester where he and his two sons, William J. and Charles H. Mayo, later established the thriving medical practice which became the world-renowned Mayo Clinic.

W. W. Mayo emigrated from England in 1845 and settled in Minnesota in 1854. Although medicine was his lifelong career, he was equally interested in politics. A man of small stature but giant energy, the "little doctor" seldom missed a chance to express his views as a devotee of Darwinism, antiprohibitionist, opponent of woman's suffrage, and antimonopolist. He served as justice of the peace at Le Sueur and mayor of Rochester, helped found the Minnesota medical society, and was elected to the state senate in 1890.

While living at Le Sueur, Dr. Mayo joined in the defense of New Ulm during the Dakota (Sioux) War of 1862, caring for the sick and wounded through a week-long siege. Refugees from the conflict flooded Le Sueur during the doctor's absence, and Mrs. Mayo and her children shared their six-room house and barn with eleven families during the crisis.

After the Mayos left Le Sueur, the home was greatly altered by a succession of owners. In 1934 it was purchased and presented to the city by Dr. Mayo's sons. It served as the Le Sueur Public Library until 1970, when it was given to the Minnesota Historical Society to be restored to its original appearance. The tiny second-floor office is furnished with medical equipment like that used by Dr. Mayo a century ago.

Located at 118 North Main Street (U.S. highway no. 169) in Le Sueur. Open daily during the summer.

W. W. MAYO HOUSE

JEFFERS PETROGLYPHS

On a lonely prairie in southwestern Minnesota, over two thousand figures and designs carved into an outcrop of red quartzite give a tantalizing glimpse of a prehistoric people only little understood by twentieth-century man. Painstakingly pecked into the rock are figures of bison, elk, bear, turtles, stick men, weapons, thunderbirds, handprints, and unrecognizable symbols which perhaps had specific meanings to the people who made them hundreds or even thousands of years ago.

Dating rock art is frustrating to modern scholars, who are forced to rely upon their identification of weapons, historic items, or stylistic forms related to historically known tribal groups. The petroglyphs at Jeffers probably were made during two periods — the Late Archaic-Early Woodland (3000 B.C. to 500 A.D.) and the Late Woodland (900-1700 A.D.). The site could have been a camping spot along a major game trail, and carving the petroglyphs may have been part of a ritual performed to assure hunting success.

Surrounding the rock outcrop is one of the few areas of virgin prairie left in Minnesota — a living museum of wild grasses and flowers presenting a changing panorama of color through the seasons. The rocks also contain geologic features of interest, including glacial striations and ripple marks resulting from wave action on an inland sea over one billion years ago. A small interpretive shelter contains exhibits about the ecology and geology of the area as well as what is known about the mysterious carvings — a surviving trace of a prehistoric people.

Located on Cottonwood County road no. 2. Accessible from U.S. highway no. 71, three miles east on county road no. 10, a mile south on county road no. 2. Open daily during the summer.

JEFFERS PETROGLYPHS

FORT RIDGELY

In the summer of 1852, Henry H. Sibley, Minnesota's first territorial representative in Congress, wrote to Winfield Scott, commanding general of the army, requesting a military post to protect settlers in the Minnesota River Valley and keep an eye on the nearby Dakota Indian reservations. Construction of a fort began the following year on a site which many of the soldiers assigned there considered "the worst place they ever beheld."

Neither well situated nor well constructed for defense, Fort Ridgely sat on high prairie ground surrounded on three sides by wooded ravines. No stockade was built, and no well was dug. In spite of these drawbacks, nine years later a group of about 180 desperate men managed to defend the fort in two critical battles which many historians consider the turning points in the Dakota (Sioux) War of 1862.

Artillery made the difference in the defense of Fort Ridgely. Several cannons had been left when regular army troops were withdrawn in 1861 for Civil War service. Well-placed cannon fire kept the Indians from storming the buildings; the Dakota had not encountered artillery fire before and it surprised and demoralized them. "But for the cannon I think we would have taken the fort," Chief Big Eagle, who participated in the second battle, said many years later.

After the war Fort Ridgely's usefulness diminished, and by 1872 all military property had been removed. When the Minnesota legislature established Fort Ridgely Memorial State Park in 1911, nearly all the structures had disappeared. The ruined stone commissary was rebuilt in the 1930s, and a log powder magazine functioning as a shed on a nearby farm was returned to the site.

Modern exhibits in the commissary illustrate life at this remote military post and describe the dramatic days in 1862 when a handful of men at an "indefensible" fort in the Minnesota Valley turned the tide of war in their favor.

Located in Fort Ridgely State Park, off state highway no. 4 six miles south of Fairfax. Open daily during the summer.

FORT RIDGELY

LOWER SIOUX AGENCY

Monuments throughout the Minnesota River Valley commemorate events of the Dakota (Sioux) War of 1862, but a more eloquent reminder of those tragic days is the stone warehouse at the Lower Sioux Agency near Morton. The only building still standing at this once thriving village, the warehouse was constructed in 1861 by Thomas J. Galbraith, the last and most inept Indian agent on the Dakota reservation before the war which killed over 600 innocent settlers and ended in exile, imprisonment, or death for the Dakota Indians of Minnesota.

The war was a culmination of years of friction between Dakota and European as white settlement pushed into Indian hunting grounds. In 1851 the Dakota gave up twenty-four million acres of land in central and western Minnesota for promised payments of about twelve and a half cents an acre and small reservations in the Minnesota Valley. Government agents and missionaries hoped the Indians could be taught to live as farmers and worship as Christians. Big Eagle, a Dakota chief, later said: "The whites were always trying to make the Indians give up their life and live like white men — go to farming, work hard and do as they did — and the Indians did not know how to do that, and did not want to anyway. It seemed too sudden to make such a change. If the Indians had tried to make the whites live like them, the whites would have resisted, and it was the same way with many Indians."

A modern interpretive center at the Lower Sioux Agency tells the story of the Dakota in Minnesota, explaining the causes and the effects as well as the events of the 1862 war. Displays begin with Dakota migration from the northern woodlands to the prairies of southwestern Minnesota during the eighteenth century and show the effects on their culture of the fur trade, the missionaries, and the treaties by which they gave up their lands. The exhibit also tells of the war's aftermath — the vengeance that fell on all Indians in southern Minnesota even though many had remained at peace, the exile of the Dakota, and the desperate battles waged on the plains until the Wounded Knee massacre in 1890. Twentieth-century reservation life and present-day Indian affairs are also discussed.

Located nine miles east of Redwood Falls on Redwood County road no. 2. Open year round.

LOWER SIOUX AGENCY

UPPER SIOUX AGENCY

The Upper Sioux Agency was established near the confluence of the Yellow Medicine and Minnesota rivers in 1854 to administer government payments and programs for the Dakota (Sioux) Indians placed on the reservation by treaties signed in 1851. Like the Lower Sioux Agency thirty miles downstream, it became a small village with homes for its employees, a warehouse, stables, a school, traders' stores, and Indian homes.

The Upper Agency was planned as a center around which Indians would establish farms. Joseph R. Brown, third of the four agents who served the reservation before 1862, was perhaps the most successful in carrying out these plans. He moved the agent's headquarters from the Lower to the Upper Agency in 1858; the same year he led a group of Dakota to Washington, D.C., and helped negotiate treaties reducing the size of the reservations by half. Brown hoped that the Indians would settle on eighty-acre farms to be allotted them from the remaining reservation land, but of the estimated 4,500 upper Dakota assigned to the reservation only about a hundred families ever became farmers. These were often harassed by the nonfarming Indians.

By 1862, frequent food shortages, delay in annuities, and trouble between farmer and non-farmer Indians set the scene for war. When it came, it broke out at the Lower Agency. Upper Agency Dakota held heated councils to decide a course of action, but could not agree on peace or war. Each individual was allowed to do as he wished. Christian Indians who opposed the war warned their white friends at the agency and helped them escape to safety. The agency buildings were sacked and burned.

After the war homesteader George E. Olds rebuilt one agency duplex for his use as a residence. Shown in the drawing opposite as Olds rebuilt it, this structure has now been restored by the Minnesota Historical Society to its prewar condition and is used as a visitors' center. Archaeologists have located the sites and foundations of the agency's other long-vanished structures, and these have been stabilized and marked.

Located in Upper Sioux Agency State Park off state highway no. 67 eight miles southeast of Granite Falls. Open daily during the summer.

UPPER SIOUX AGENCY

MILLE LACS INDIAN MUSEUM

"Mde wakan" — spirit lake or wonderful lake — was the name by which the Dakota (Sioux) Indians knew the big lake that was the center of their woodland home for generations before French voyageurs and traders christened the region "Mille Lacs" (thousand lakes). The Dakota controlled a vast forested area of northern Minnesota between the Red River and Lake Superior, and one band of that tribe was called Mdewakanton — "people of the wonderful lake."

By the early eighteenth century, the growth of the fur trade and the arrival of Europeans in the Northwest had upset long-established relationships among many Indian groups, including the Dakota and the Chippewa (Ojibway) who lived to the northeast. Soon the Chippewa, armed with muskets obtained from traders, pushed westward in search of new hunting grounds. Dakota and Chippewa fought intermittently for many years. About 1745, according to an Indian historian, a three-day battle at Mille Lacs Lake established the Chippewa in the region, where many of their descendants still live. The Dakota retreated south and west, changing their way of life to meet the challenges of a prairie environment. With the help of horses and guns, they soon became skilled buffalo hunters.

The Mille Lacs Indian Museum tells the story of the region's Indian inhabitants. Displays compare the life styles of Dakota and Chippewa, describe the arrival of the fur traders, and explain the effects of the three-day battle on both Indian groups. Life-size dioramas portray Chippewa life in each of the four seasons. The two drawings opposite show winter and summer settings. The painted backgrounds of these exhibits blend into detailed foreground scenes containing trees, shrubs, and bark- and grass-covered lodges stocked with the utensils made and used by the Chippewa before white settlement drastically changed their centuries-old woodland tradition.

Located on U.S. highway no. 169 near Vineland. Open daily during the summer.

MILLE LACS INDIAN MUSEUM

NORTH WEST COMPANY FUR POST

From the seventeenth to the early nineteenth centuries fur traders from three nations paddled canoes through Minnesota's lakes and rivers in pursuit of rich pelts bartered by the Indians. In the autumn of 1804 one such trader and his crew, employees of the British North West Company, built a small wintering post on the bank of the Snake River and spent the season trading with the nearby Ojibway Indians.

Like other company traders, this man kept a diary. For many years it was thought to be the record left by Thomas Connor, but recent evidence suggests that John Sayer, chief of the company's Fond du Lac department, was the author. The journal describes the building of the post in six weeks, the progress of the trade, the constant search for provisions, and the usual monotony and rare drama of a wilderness winter. In April, 1805, the trader and his crew packed their accumulation of muskrat, deer, bear, and beaver skins and departed for a collection point on Lake Superior. Whether he or anyone else ever used the post again is not known.

In 1964 the site of this long-vanished wintering post was discovered through the presence of a large number of fur trade artifacts found in a plowed field. Four summers of careful investigation by archaeologists uncovered evidence of a six-room log cabin surrounded by a stockade with two corner bastions. Three additional summers were required for the Minnesota Historical Society to reconstruct the post and stock it with replicas of the everyday utensils and trade goods used by the voyageurs.

Gaily costumed guides at the reconstructed North West Company Fur Post demonstrate the daily activities and tell the story of the colorful men of the fur trade, who, at this site and hundreds of similar outposts, carried on for over two centuries the difficult and occasionally romantic business that opened up a continent.

Located on Pine County road no. 7, about 1.5 miles west of Interstate highway no. 35. Open daily during the summer.

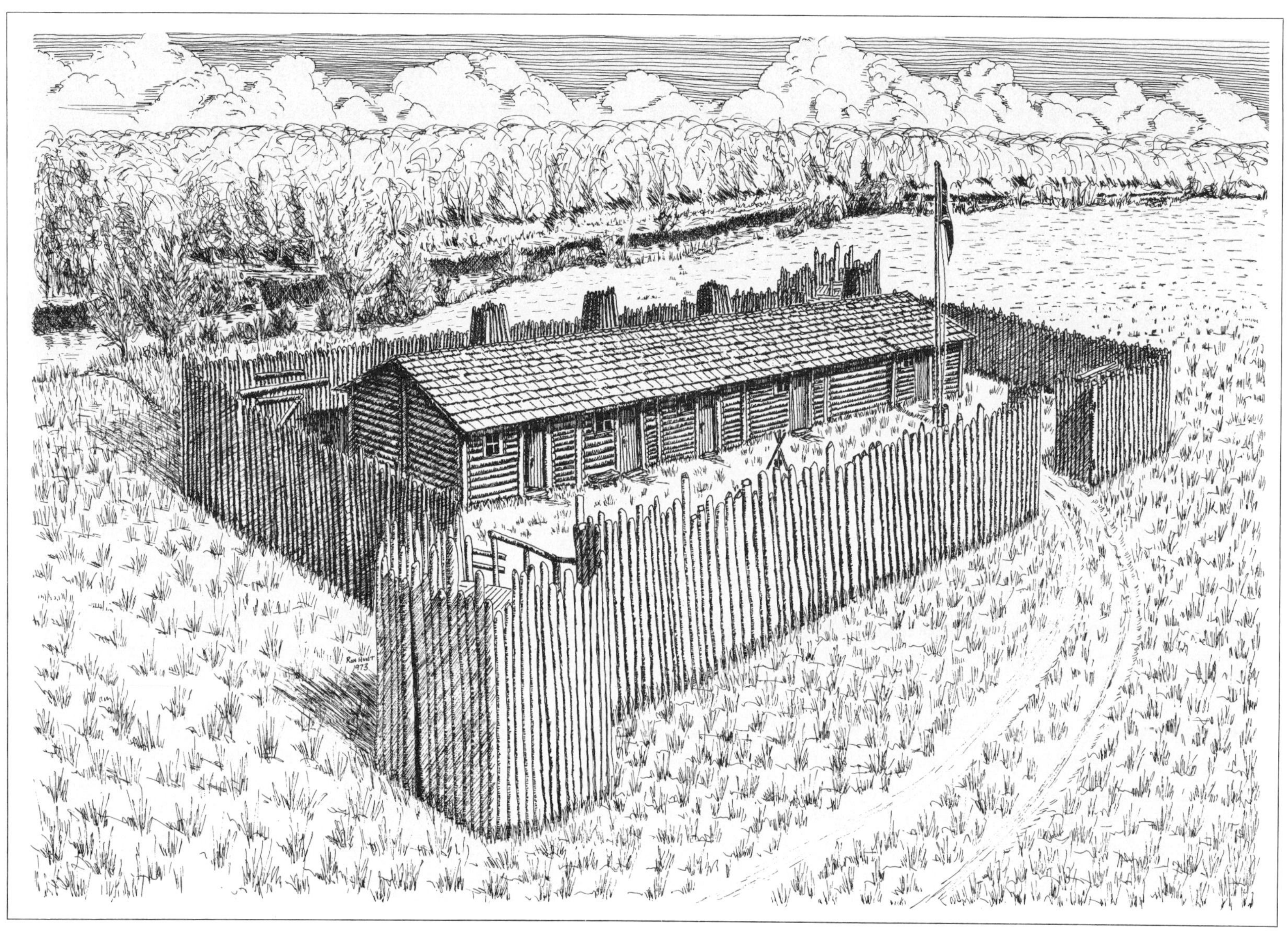

NORTH WEST COMPANY FUR POST

W. H. C. FOLSOM HOUSE

"Angel's Hill" was the derisive name applied by some residents of Taylors Falls to the area around the Methodist Church built high on a hill above the commercial district. There, in the mid-nineteenth century, early St. Croix Valley settlers re-created a New England village of white pine houses, many of them in the Federal-Greek Revival style. One of the first of these homes was built in 1855 by William Henry Carman Folsom, an enterprising lumberman from Maine actively involved in the business and community life of the valley.

Folsom had traveled as a youth of nineteen to Wisconsin Territory in 1836 and in nine years had saved the capital he needed to begin operations as an independent logger in the fast-growing white pine industry. He moved to Stillwater in 1845 and to Taylors Falls in 1850. There he opened a general store and purchased a quarter interest in the infant townsite. Soon his civic interests led him into politics; he was a member of the 1857 constitutional convention and served several terms in the Minnesota legislature.

Although most of the outbuildings Folsom built have disappeared, his house has changed relatively little in over a century. In 1968 the state of Minnesota purchased the home and many of its original furnishings from Stanley Folsom, the builder's grandson. The entire Angel's Hill district, today a handsome collection of well-maintained and actively used buildings, was placed on the National Register of Historic Places in 1972.

Located on Government Road in Taylors Falls. Open daily during the summer.

W. H. C. FOLSOM HOUSE

OLIVER H. KELLEY FARM

"We want to bring in the whole farming community, — get the brains inside the vineyard, then put ideas into the brains — set them to thinking — let them feel that they are human beings, and the strength of the nation, their labor honorable, and farming the highest calling on earth." Thus Oliver Hudson Kelley expressed his hopes for the new National Grange of the Order of the Patrons of Husbandry, which he and six associates organized in 1867 "to advance education, to elevate and dignify the occupation of the farmer, and to protect its members against the numerous combinations by which their interests are injuriously affected."

Oliver H. Kelley arrived in Minnesota Territory in 1849 and homesteaded this farm on the Mississippi River one year later. Besides farming, which Kelley did "by the book," he contributed articles to farm journals and newspapers, wrote reports for the United States Bureau of Agriculture, and interested himself in local politics, claiming "to be as full of pub-

lic spirit as a dog is full of fleas." He was also active in Minnesota's first Masonic lodge.

After founding the national farm fraternity, Kelley worked from his farm home organizing local granges. By 1869 Minnesota had the nation's first state grange as well as thirty-seven active local granges. Late in 1870, Kelley moved to Washington, D.C., where he continued to serve as executive secretary of the National Grange until his retirement in 1878.

The Kelley Farm is now known as the "birthplace of organized agriculture in the United States" and is a registered National Historic Landmark. The farmhouse now on the property was completed sometime after 1870; it was restored as a mid-Victorian farm home by the National Grange in the 1950s. In 1961 the Grange presented the 190-acre farm to the Minnesota Historical Society, which is developing it as a working farm of the 1860–70 era.

Located two miles southeast of Elk River on U.S. highways nos. 169, 10, and 52. Open daily during the summer.

OLIVER H. KELLEY FARM

CHARLES A. LINDBERGH HOUSE

"I never deserted the farm as the ultimate goal for my return — and there is my home when I am home, for the farm unquestionably is the best of all places to live, and it affords the most independence," wrote Charles A. Lindbergh, Sr., about his home on the bank of the Mississippi River near Little Falls.

Although Lindbergh praised the "independence" of farm life, he never worked as a farmer during his adult life. A successful attorney and businessman, he was deeply interested in the economic conditions that produced hardships for his farm neighbors. Much of his public career was devoted to efforts to expose the "money trust" of big banking and industry which he felt was exploiting small farmers, laborers, and businessmen.

Lindbergh served in Congress from 1907 until 1917 as an outspoken and hard-working Progressive Republican whom one of his colleagues called "the most sanely radical man I ever met." In the Republican primary election of 1918 he ran for governor of Minnesota with the backing of the Nonpartisan League, an agrarian protest movement and the forerunner of the Farmer-Labor party. He lost that election, one of the state's bitterest, as he did a race for the U.S. senate in 1922. Lindbergh died in 1924, while he was once again a candidate for governor.

Charles A. Lindbergh, Jr., who would win world acclaim in 1927 as the first man to fly alone and nonstop from New York to Paris, spent most of his boyhood summers on this farm. As a teenager he managed the place for three years, then left it in 1920 to enroll in college before beginning his aviation career. After Charles left, the house stood empty, and in 1927 it was virtually stripped by souvenir hunters. In 1931 the family gave the house and the 110-acre farm to the state of Minnesota as a memorial to Charles A. Lindbergh, Sr.

The Minnesota Historical Society recently restored the house with assistance from Charles Lindbergh, Jr., who provided detailed descriptions of its 1906–1920 appearance. An interpretive center near the house contains exhibits telling the story of three generations of Lindberghs, including August, grandfather of the aviator, who served in the Swedish parliament before coming to the United States as a homesteader in 1859.

Located in Charles A. Lindbergh State Park on Lindbergh Drive (Morrison County road no. 52) south of Little Falls. Open daily during the summer. Interpretive Center open year round.

CHARLES A. LINDBERGH HOUSE

15 HISTORIC PLACES IN MINNESOTA

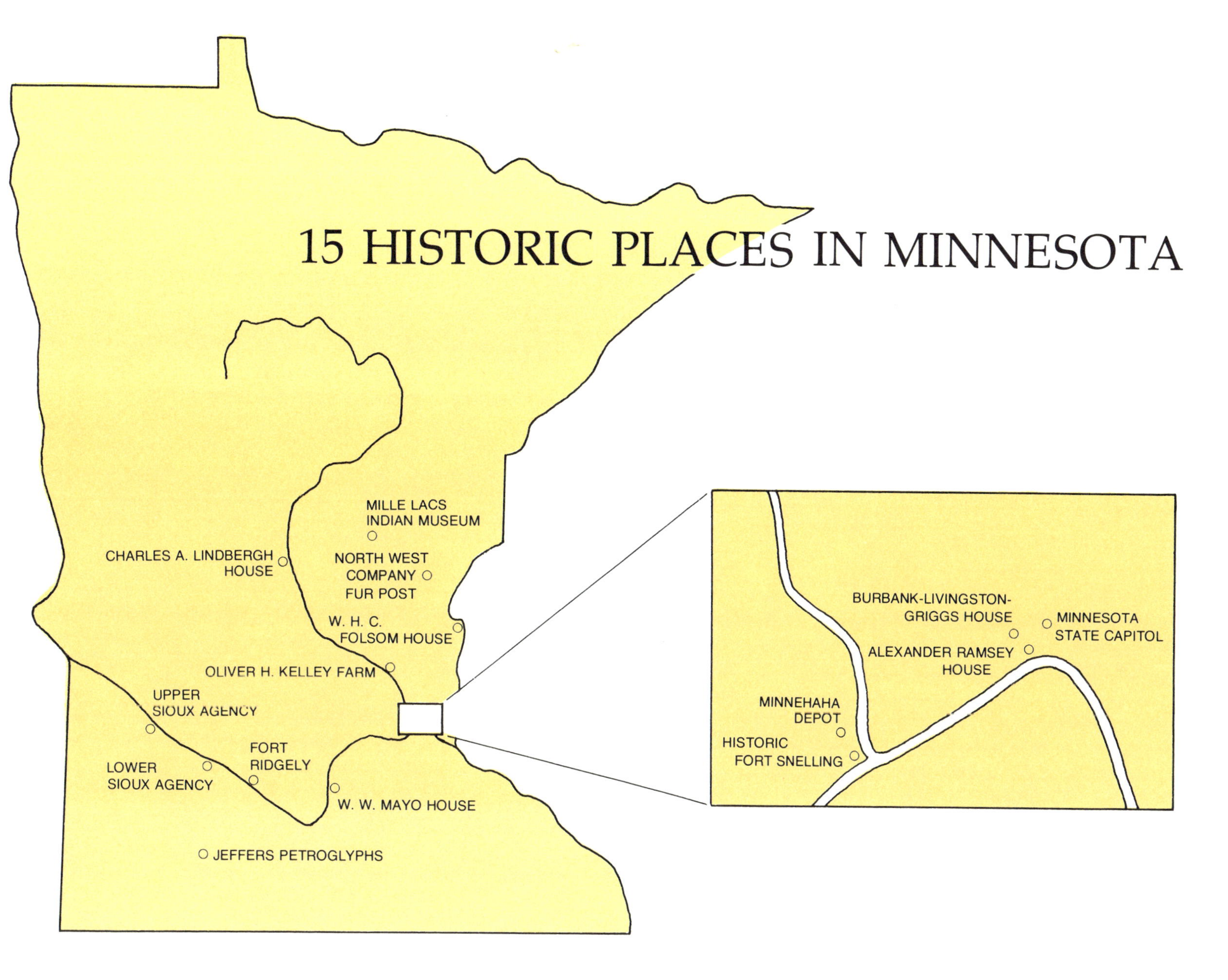

MINNESOTA HISTORIC SITES PAMPHLET SERIES

MINNESOTA HISTORICAL SOCIETY, 1500 MISSISSIPPI STREET, ST. PAUL, MINNESOTA 55101